# 50 Delicious Ramen Dishes for Home

By: Kelly Johnson

# Table of Contents

- Classic Shoyu Ramen
- Tonkotsu Ramen
- Miso Ramen
- Shio Ramen
- Spicy Miso Ramen
- Black Garlic Ramen
- Chicken Paitan Ramen
- Curry Ramen
- Tantanmen (Spicy Sesame Ramen)
- Vegan Miso Ramen
- Seafood Ramen
- Kimchi Ramen
- Spicy Beef Ramen
- Shoyu Butter Corn Ramen
- Chashu Pork Ramen
- Yakibuta Ramen (Grilled Pork Ramen)
- Mushroom Ramen
- Smoked Duck Ramen
- Shrimp Tempura Ramen
- Bacon and Egg Breakfast Ramen
- Cheese Ramen
- Soy Milk Ramen
- Garlic Butter Ramen
- Spicy Tofu Ramen
- Clam Ramen
- Yuzu Shio Ramen
- Teriyaki Chicken Ramen
- Lobster Ramen
- Thai Coconut Curry Ramen
- BBQ Pork Ramen
- Cold Tsukemen (Dipping Ramen)
- Black Pepper Beef Ramen
- Charred Scallion Ramen
- Spicy Gochujang Ramen
- Roasted Tomato Ramen

- Chicken and Ginger Ramen
- Truffle Oil Ramen
- Caramelized Onion Ramen
- Spicy Peanut Butter Ramen
- Szechuan Peppercorn Ramen
- Duck Fat Ramen
- Umami Mushroom Broth Ramen
- Pork Belly and Egg Ramen
- Chilled Summer Ramen
- Sesame Garlic Ramen
- Kimchi and Spam Ramen
- Japanese Curry Ramen
- BBQ Brisket Ramen
- Five-Spice Chicken Ramen
- Oyster Mushroom Ramen

## Classic Shoyu Ramen

**Ingredients:**

**Broth:**

- 4 cups chicken or pork broth
- 1/4 cup soy sauce
- 1 tbsp mirin
- 1 tsp sesame oil
- 1 clove garlic, minced
- 1-inch ginger, sliced

**Toppings:**

- 2 soft-boiled eggs
- 2 slices chashu pork or grilled chicken
- 1/2 cup bamboo shoots
- 1/4 cup sliced green onions
- 1 sheet nori

**Noodles:**

- 2 servings fresh ramen noodles

**Instructions:**

1. In a pot, combine broth, soy sauce, mirin, sesame oil, garlic, and ginger. Simmer for 15 minutes.
2. Cook ramen noodles according to package instructions. Drain and divide into bowls.
3. Strain broth and pour over noodles.
4. Top with eggs, pork, bamboo shoots, green onions, and nori. Serve hot.

**Tonkotsu Ramen**

**Ingredients:**

**Broth:**

- 4 lbs pork bones
- 8 cups water
- 1 onion, halved
- 4 cloves garlic
- 1-inch ginger, sliced
- 1/4 cup soy sauce
- 1 tbsp mirin

**Toppings:**

- Chashu pork slices
- Soft-boiled eggs
- Green onions
- Wood ear mushrooms
- Nori

**Noodles:**

- 2 servings fresh ramen noodles

**Instructions:**

1. Boil pork bones for 10 minutes, drain, and rinse.
2. Refill with fresh water and add onion, garlic, and ginger. Simmer for 8-10 hours.
3. Strain the broth and season with soy sauce and mirin.
4. Cook ramen noodles, then assemble with broth and toppings.

## Miso Ramen

**Ingredients:**

**Broth:**

- 4 cups chicken broth
- 2 tbsp miso paste
- 1 tbsp soy sauce
- 1 tsp sesame oil
- 1 clove garlic, minced
- 1-inch ginger, grated

**Toppings:**

- Ground pork or tofu
- Corn kernels
- Soft-boiled eggs
- Green onions
- Butter

**Noodles:**

- 2 servings fresh ramen noodles

**Instructions:**

1. Sauté garlic and ginger in sesame oil. Add miso paste and cook for 1 minute.
2. Stir in broth and soy sauce, simmer for 10 minutes.
3. Cook ramen noodles, then divide into bowls.
4. Pour broth over noodles and top with pork, eggs, corn, butter, and green onions.

**Shio Ramen**

**Ingredients:**

**Broth:**

- 4 cups chicken broth
- 1 tbsp sea salt
- 1 tsp fish sauce
- 1 tbsp sake
- 1 clove garlic, minced
- 1-inch ginger, sliced

**Toppings:**

- Chicken slices
- Green onions
- Bamboo shoots
- Soft-boiled egg

**Noodles:**

- 2 servings fresh ramen noodles

**Instructions:**

1. In a pot, mix broth, salt, fish sauce, sake, garlic, and ginger. Simmer for 15 minutes.
2. Cook ramen noodles and divide into bowls.
3. Pour hot broth over noodles and top with chicken, green onions, bamboo shoots, and egg.

**Spicy Miso Ramen**

**Ingredients:**

**Broth:**

- 4 cups chicken broth
- 2 tbsp miso paste
- 1 tbsp soy sauce
- 1 tbsp chili paste (or to taste)
- 1 clove garlic, minced
- 1-inch ginger, grated

**Toppings:**

- Spicy ground pork
- Corn
- Soft-boiled egg
- Green onions
- Chili oil

**Noodles:**

- 2 servings fresh ramen noodles

**Instructions:**

1. Sauté garlic and ginger in sesame oil. Stir in miso and chili paste.
2. Add broth and soy sauce, then simmer for 10 minutes.
3. Cook noodles and divide into bowls.
4. Pour broth over noodles and top with spicy pork, egg, corn, and green onions. Drizzle with chili oil.

**Black Garlic Ramen**

**Ingredients:**

**Broth:**

- 4 cups pork broth
- 1 tbsp soy sauce
- 1 tbsp black garlic oil

**Toppings:**

- Chashu pork
- Soft-boiled egg
- Green onions
- Fried garlic chips

**Noodles:**

- 2 servings fresh ramen noodles

**Instructions:**

1. Heat pork broth and season with soy sauce.
2. Cook noodles and divide into bowls.
3. Pour broth over noodles, top with pork, egg, green onions, and garlic chips.
4. Drizzle black garlic oil on top before serving.

# Chicken Paitan Ramen

**Ingredients:**

**Broth:**

- 4 cups chicken broth
- 1 tbsp soy sauce
- 1/2 cup milk

**Toppings:**

- Sliced chicken breast
- Soft-boiled egg
- Green onions

**Noodles:**

- 2 servings fresh ramen noodles

**Instructions:**

1. Heat chicken broth and add soy sauce and milk. Simmer for 10 minutes.
2. Cook noodles and divide into bowls.
3. Pour broth over noodles and add chicken, egg, and green onions.

## Curry Ramen

**Ingredients:**

**Broth:**

- 4 cups chicken broth
- 2 tbsp Japanese curry paste
- 1 tbsp soy sauce
- 1/2 cup coconut milk

**Toppings:**

- Grilled chicken
- Soft-boiled egg
- Green onions
- Pickled ginger

**Noodles:**

- 2 servings fresh ramen noodles

**Instructions:**

1. Heat broth and whisk in curry paste, soy sauce, and coconut milk.
2. Simmer for 10 minutes.
3. Cook noodles and divide into bowls.
4. Pour broth over noodles, then add toppings.

## Tantanmen (Spicy Sesame Ramen)

**Ingredients:**

**Broth:**

- 4 cups chicken broth
- 2 tbsp sesame paste
- 1 tbsp soy sauce
- 1 tbsp chili oil

**Toppings:**

- Spicy ground pork
- Soft-boiled egg
- Green onions
- Bok choy

**Noodles:**

- 2 servings fresh ramen noodles

**Instructions:**

1. Heat broth and whisk in sesame paste, soy sauce, and chili oil.
2. Cook noodles and divide into bowls.
3. Pour broth over noodles and top with pork, egg, and bok choy.

**Vegan Miso Ramen**

**Ingredients:**

**Broth:**

- 4 cups vegetable broth
- 2 tbsp miso paste
- 1 tbsp soy sauce
- 1 tsp sesame oil
- 1 clove garlic, minced

**Toppings:**

- Tofu cubes
- Corn
- Mushrooms
- Green onions

**Noodles:**

- 2 servings ramen noodles

**Instructions:**

1. Heat vegetable broth and whisk in miso, soy sauce, sesame oil, and garlic.
2. Cook noodles and divide into bowls.
3. Pour broth over noodles and add tofu, corn, mushrooms, and green onions.

## Seafood Ramen

**Ingredients:**

**Broth:**

- 4 cups seafood or chicken broth
- 1 tbsp soy sauce
- 1 tbsp miso paste
- 1 tsp sesame oil
- 1 clove garlic, minced
- 1-inch ginger, sliced

**Toppings:**

- Shrimp, squid, and scallops
- Soft-boiled egg
- Nori
- Green onions
- Bean sprouts

**Noodles:**

- 2 servings fresh ramen noodles

**Instructions:**

1. Heat broth and whisk in soy sauce, miso paste, sesame oil, garlic, and ginger. Simmer for 10 minutes.
2. Cook seafood in the broth for 3-5 minutes. Remove and set aside.
3. Cook ramen noodles and divide into bowls.
4. Pour broth over noodles and add seafood and toppings.

**Kimchi Ramen**

**Ingredients:**

**Broth:**

- 4 cups chicken broth
- 1 cup chopped kimchi
- 1 tbsp gochujang (Korean chili paste)
- 1 tbsp soy sauce
- 1 tsp sesame oil
- 1 clove garlic, minced

**Toppings:**

- Soft-boiled egg
- Sliced pork or tofu
- Green onions
- Nori

**Noodles:**

- 2 servings fresh ramen noodles

**Instructions:**

1. Heat broth and add kimchi, gochujang, soy sauce, sesame oil, and garlic. Simmer for 10 minutes.
2. Cook ramen noodles and divide into bowls.
3. Pour broth over noodles and add toppings.

**Spicy Beef Ramen**

**Ingredients:**

**Broth:**

- 4 cups beef broth
- 1 tbsp chili paste
- 1 tbsp soy sauce
- 1 tsp sesame oil
- 1 clove garlic, minced
- 1-inch ginger, grated

**Toppings:**

- Thinly sliced beef
- Soft-boiled egg
- Green onions
- Chili oil

**Noodles:**

- 2 servings fresh ramen noodles

**Instructions:**

1. Heat broth and whisk in chili paste, soy sauce, sesame oil, garlic, and ginger.
2. Add beef and cook for 3 minutes until tender. Remove and set aside.
3. Cook ramen noodles and divide into bowls.
4. Pour broth over noodles and add beef and toppings.

**Shoyu Butter Corn Ramen**

**Ingredients:**

**Broth:**

- 4 cups chicken broth
- 1/4 cup soy sauce
- 1 tbsp mirin
- 1 tbsp butter

**Toppings:**

- Corn kernels
- Soft-boiled egg
- Green onions
- Nori

**Noodles:**

- 2 servings fresh ramen noodles

**Instructions:**

1. Heat broth and stir in soy sauce, mirin, and butter.
2. Cook ramen noodles and divide into bowls.
3. Pour broth over noodles and top with corn, egg, and green onions.

## Chashu Pork Ramen

**Ingredients:**

**Broth:**

- 4 cups pork broth
- 1 tbsp soy sauce
- 1 tbsp mirin
- 1 tsp sesame oil

**Toppings:**

- Slices of chashu pork
- Soft-boiled egg
- Green onions
- Nori

**Noodles:**

- 2 servings fresh ramen noodles

**Instructions:**

1. Heat broth and season with soy sauce, mirin, and sesame oil.
2. Cook ramen noodles and divide into bowls.
3. Pour broth over noodles and top with chashu, egg, green onions, and nori.

## Yakibuta Ramen (Grilled Pork Ramen)

**Ingredients:**

**Broth:**

- 4 cups chicken or pork broth
- 1 tbsp soy sauce
- 1 tbsp sake
- 1 tsp sesame oil

**Toppings:**

- Grilled pork belly slices
- Soft-boiled egg
- Green onions
- Bamboo shoots

**Noodles:**

- 2 servings fresh ramen noodles

**Instructions:**

1. Grill pork belly until caramelized and crispy.
2. Heat broth and season with soy sauce, sake, and sesame oil.
3. Cook ramen noodles and divide into bowls.
4. Pour broth over noodles and add grilled pork and toppings.

# Mushroom Ramen

**Ingredients:**

**Broth:**

- 4 cups vegetable broth
- 1 tbsp soy sauce
- 1 tbsp miso paste
- 1 tsp sesame oil
- 1 cup mixed mushrooms (shiitake, enoki, cremini)

**Toppings:**

- Tofu or soft-boiled egg
- Green onions
- Nori

**Noodles:**

- 2 servings fresh ramen noodles

**Instructions:**

1. Sauté mushrooms in sesame oil until tender.
2. Heat broth and whisk in soy sauce and miso paste.
3. Cook ramen noodles and divide into bowls.
4. Pour broth over noodles and add mushrooms and toppings.

**Smoked Duck Ramen**

**Ingredients:**

**Broth:**

- 4 cups chicken broth
- 1 tbsp soy sauce
- 1 tbsp mirin

**Toppings:**

- Slices of smoked duck
- Soft-boiled egg
- Green onions
- Bamboo shoots

**Noodles:**

- 2 servings fresh ramen noodles

**Instructions:**

1. Heat broth and season with soy sauce and mirin.
2. Cook ramen noodles and divide into bowls.
3. Pour broth over noodles and top with smoked duck and other toppings.

## Shrimp Tempura Ramen

**Ingredients:**

**Broth:**

- 4 cups dashi broth
- 1 tbsp soy sauce
- 1 tsp sesame oil

**Toppings:**

- Shrimp tempura
- Green onions
- Soft-boiled egg

**Noodles:**

- 2 servings fresh ramen noodles

**Instructions:**

1. Heat broth and season with soy sauce and sesame oil.
2. Cook ramen noodles and divide into bowls.
3. Pour broth over noodles and top with shrimp tempura and toppings.

**Bacon and Egg Breakfast Ramen**

**Ingredients:**

**Broth:**

- 4 cups chicken broth
- 1 tbsp soy sauce
- 1 tsp butter

**Toppings:**

- Crispy bacon
- Soft-boiled egg
- Green onions

**Noodles:**

- 2 servings fresh ramen noodles

**Instructions:**

1. Heat broth and whisk in soy sauce and butter.
2. Cook ramen noodles and divide into bowls.
3. Pour broth over noodles and top with bacon, egg, and green onions.

**Cheese Ramen**

**Ingredients:**

**Broth:**

- 4 cups chicken broth
- 1/2 cup milk
- 1/2 cup shredded cheddar or mozzarella cheese
- 1 tbsp soy sauce
- 1 tsp butter

**Toppings:**

- Soft-boiled egg
- Extra shredded cheese
- Green onions

**Noodles:**

- 2 servings fresh ramen noodles

**Instructions:**

1. Heat broth and whisk in milk, cheese, soy sauce, and butter until smooth.
2. Cook ramen noodles and divide into bowls.
3. Pour broth over noodles and top with egg, cheese, and green onions.

**Soy Milk Ramen**

**Ingredients:**

**Broth:**

- 3 cups vegetable or chicken broth
- 1 cup unsweetened soy milk
- 1 tbsp miso paste
- 1 tbsp soy sauce
- 1 tsp sesame oil

**Toppings:**

- Tofu cubes
- Soft-boiled egg
- Green onions
- Mushrooms

**Noodles:**

- 2 servings fresh ramen noodles

**Instructions:**

1. Heat broth and stir in soy milk, miso paste, soy sauce, and sesame oil.
2. Cook ramen noodles and divide into bowls.
3. Pour broth over noodles and add tofu, egg, and mushrooms.

**Garlic Butter Ramen**

**Ingredients:**

**Broth:**

- 4 cups chicken broth
- 3 cloves garlic, minced
- 1 tbsp soy sauce
- 1 tbsp butter

**Toppings:**

- Soft-boiled egg
- Sautéed mushrooms
- Green onions

**Noodles:**

- 2 servings fresh ramen noodles

**Instructions:**

1. Sauté garlic in butter until fragrant.
2. Add broth and soy sauce, then simmer for 10 minutes.
3. Cook ramen noodles and divide into bowls.
4. Pour broth over noodles and add toppings.

**Spicy Tofu Ramen**

**Ingredients:**

**Broth:**

- 4 cups vegetable broth
- 1 tbsp gochujang (Korean chili paste)
- 1 tbsp soy sauce
- 1 tsp sesame oil
- 1 clove garlic, minced

**Toppings:**

- Tofu cubes
- Soft-boiled egg
- Green onions
- Chili oil

**Noodles:**

- 2 servings fresh ramen noodles

**Instructions:**

1. Heat broth and stir in gochujang, soy sauce, sesame oil, and garlic.
2. Cook ramen noodles and divide into bowls.
3. Pour broth over noodles and add tofu, egg, and green onions.
4. Drizzle with chili oil before serving.

## Clam Ramen

**Ingredients:**

**Broth:**

- 4 cups seafood broth
- 1 cup fresh clams
- 1 tbsp soy sauce
- 1 tbsp sake

**Toppings:**

- Fresh clams
- Green onions
- Soft-boiled egg

**Noodles:**

- 2 servings fresh ramen noodles

**Instructions:**

1. Steam clams in sake until they open, then add broth and soy sauce.
2. Cook ramen noodles and divide into bowls.
3. Pour broth over noodles and top with clams, egg, and green onions.

**Yuzu Shio Ramen**

**Ingredients:**

**Broth:**

- 4 cups chicken broth
- 1 tbsp yuzu juice
- 1 tsp sea salt
- 1 tsp soy sauce

**Toppings:**

- Chicken slices
- Green onions
- Soft-boiled egg

**Noodles:**

- 2 servings fresh ramen noodles

**Instructions:**

1. Heat broth and stir in yuzu juice, salt, and soy sauce.
2. Cook ramen noodles and divide into bowls.
3. Pour broth over noodles and add chicken, egg, and green onions.

**Teriyaki Chicken Ramen**

**Ingredients:**

**Broth:**

- 4 cups chicken broth
- 1 tbsp soy sauce
- 1 tbsp teriyaki sauce

**Toppings:**

- Teriyaki-glazed chicken slices
- Soft-boiled egg
- Green onions

**Noodles:**

- 2 servings fresh ramen noodles

**Instructions:**

1. Cook chicken in teriyaki sauce until glazed.
2. Heat broth and add soy sauce and teriyaki sauce.
3. Cook ramen noodles and divide into bowls.
4. Pour broth over noodles and add teriyaki chicken and toppings.

## Lobster Ramen

**Ingredients:**

**Broth:**

- 4 cups seafood broth
- 1 tbsp miso paste
- 1 tbsp soy sauce

**Toppings:**

- Lobster meat
- Soft-boiled egg
- Green onions

**Noodles:**

- 2 servings fresh ramen noodles

**Instructions:**

1. Heat broth and stir in miso paste and soy sauce.
2. Cook lobster in broth for 5 minutes, then remove.
3. Cook ramen noodles and divide into bowls.
4. Pour broth over noodles and add lobster and toppings.

**Thai Coconut Curry Ramen**

**Ingredients:**

**Broth:**

- 3 cups chicken broth
- 1 cup coconut milk
- 1 tbsp Thai red curry paste
- 1 tbsp fish sauce

**Toppings:**

- Grilled shrimp or chicken
- Soft-boiled egg
- Cilantro

**Noodles:**

- 2 servings fresh ramen noodles

**Instructions:**

1. Heat broth and whisk in coconut milk, curry paste, and fish sauce.
2. Cook ramen noodles and divide into bowls.
3. Pour broth over noodles and add shrimp or chicken and toppings.

**BBQ Pork Ramen**

**Ingredients:**

**Broth:**

- 4 cups pork broth
- 1 tbsp soy sauce
- 1 tbsp hoisin sauce

**Toppings:**

- BBQ pork slices
- Soft-boiled egg
- Green onions

**Noodles:**

- 2 servings fresh ramen noodles

**Instructions:**

1. Heat broth and stir in soy sauce and hoisin sauce.
2. Cook ramen noodles and divide into bowls.
3. Pour broth over noodles and add BBQ pork and toppings.

## Cold Tsukemen (Dipping Ramen)

**Ingredients:**

**Dipping Sauce:**

- 2 cups dashi or chicken broth
- 2 tbsp soy sauce
- 1 tbsp mirin
- 1 tsp sesame oil
- 1/2 tsp grated ginger

**Toppings:**

- Chashu pork slices
- Soft-boiled egg
- Nori
- Green onions

**Noodles:**

- 2 servings fresh ramen noodles

**Instructions:**

1. Mix dipping sauce ingredients in a pot and simmer for 5 minutes. Let cool.
2. Cook ramen noodles, rinse under cold water, and drain.
3. Serve noodles cold with dipping sauce and toppings on the side.

**Black Pepper Beef Ramen**

**Ingredients:**

**Broth:**

- 4 cups beef broth
- 1 tbsp soy sauce
- 1 tsp black pepper
- 1 clove garlic, minced

**Toppings:**

- Thinly sliced beef
- Soft-boiled egg
- Green onions
- Crushed black pepper

**Noodles:**

- 2 servings fresh ramen noodles

**Instructions:**

1. Heat broth and whisk in soy sauce, black pepper, and garlic.
2. Cook beef slices in the broth for 2 minutes. Remove and set aside.
3. Cook ramen noodles and divide into bowls.
4. Pour broth over noodles and top with beef, egg, and green onions.

## Charred Scallion Ramen

**Ingredients:**

**Broth:**

- 4 cups chicken broth
- 1 tbsp soy sauce
- 1 tsp sesame oil

**Toppings:**

- Charred scallions (grilled or pan-seared)
- Soft-boiled egg
- Sesame seeds
- Nori

**Noodles:**

- 2 servings fresh ramen noodles

**Instructions:**

1. Heat broth and stir in soy sauce and sesame oil.
2. Char scallions on a grill or stovetop until slightly blackened.
3. Cook ramen noodles and divide into bowls.
4. Pour broth over noodles and top with charred scallions and other toppings.

**Spicy Gochujang Ramen**

**Ingredients:**

**Broth:**

- 4 cups chicken broth
- 1 tbsp gochujang (Korean chili paste)
- 1 tbsp soy sauce
- 1 tsp sesame oil
- 1 clove garlic, minced

**Toppings:**

- Soft-boiled egg
- Green onions
- Tofu or sliced pork

**Noodles:**

- 2 servings fresh ramen noodles

**Instructions:**

1. Heat broth and whisk in gochujang, soy sauce, sesame oil, and garlic.
2. Cook ramen noodles and divide into bowls.
3. Pour broth over noodles and top with egg, tofu, and green onions.

## Roasted Tomato Ramen

**Ingredients:**

**Broth:**

- 4 cups vegetable broth
- 2 roasted tomatoes, blended
- 1 tbsp soy sauce
- 1 tsp olive oil

**Toppings:**

- Charred cherry tomatoes
- Soft-boiled egg
- Green onions

**Noodles:**

- 2 servings fresh ramen noodles

**Instructions:**

1. Roast tomatoes in the oven at 400°F (200°C) for 20 minutes, then blend into a purée.
2. Heat broth and stir in tomato purée, soy sauce, and olive oil.
3. Cook ramen noodles and divide into bowls.
4. Pour broth over noodles and top with cherry tomatoes and other toppings.

**Chicken and Ginger Ramen**

**Ingredients:**

**Broth:**

- 4 cups chicken broth
- 1-inch ginger, grated
- 1 tbsp soy sauce

**Toppings:**

- Sliced chicken breast
- Soft-boiled egg
- Green onions

**Noodles:**

- 2 servings fresh ramen noodles

**Instructions:**

1. Heat broth and stir in ginger and soy sauce. Simmer for 10 minutes.
2. Cook ramen noodles and divide into bowls.
3. Pour broth over noodles and add chicken, egg, and green onions.

## Truffle Oil Ramen

**Ingredients:**

**Broth:**

- 4 cups chicken or mushroom broth
- 1 tbsp soy sauce
- 1 tsp truffle oil

**Toppings:**

- Sautéed mushrooms
- Soft-boiled egg
- Green onions

**Noodles:**

- 2 servings fresh ramen noodles

**Instructions:**

1. Heat broth and stir in soy sauce and truffle oil.
2. Cook ramen noodles and divide into bowls.
3. Pour broth over noodles and top with mushrooms, egg, and green onions.

## Caramelized Onion Ramen

**Ingredients:**

**Broth:**

- 4 cups beef broth
- 2 onions, caramelized
- 1 tbsp soy sauce
- 1 tsp butter

**Toppings:**

- Soft-boiled egg
- Sautéed onions
- Green onions

**Noodles:**

- 2 servings fresh ramen noodles

**Instructions:**

1. Cook onions in butter over low heat until caramelized (about 20 minutes).
2. Heat broth and stir in caramelized onions and soy sauce.
3. Cook ramen noodles and divide into bowls.
4. Pour broth over noodles and top with extra onions and toppings.

**Spicy Peanut Butter Ramen**

**Ingredients:**

**Broth:**

- 4 cups chicken broth
- 2 tbsp peanut butter
- 1 tbsp soy sauce
- 1 tbsp chili paste
- 1 tsp sesame oil

**Toppings:**

- Crushed peanuts
- Soft-boiled egg
- Green onions

**Noodles:**

- 2 servings fresh ramen noodles

**Instructions:**

1. Heat broth and whisk in peanut butter, soy sauce, chili paste, and sesame oil.
2. Cook ramen noodles and divide into bowls.
3. Pour broth over noodles and top with crushed peanuts and other toppings.

**Szechuan Peppercorn Ramen**

**Ingredients:**

**Broth:**

- 4 cups beef broth
- 1 tbsp soy sauce
- 1 tsp Szechuan peppercorns, crushed

**Toppings:**

- Sliced beef
- Green onions
- Soft-boiled egg

**Noodles:**

- 2 servings fresh ramen noodles

**Instructions:**

1. Heat broth and stir in soy sauce and Szechuan peppercorns. Simmer for 10 minutes.
2. Cook ramen noodles and divide into bowls.
3. Pour broth over noodles and top with beef, egg, and green onions.

**Duck Fat Ramen**

**Ingredients:**

**Broth:**

- 4 cups chicken broth
- 2 tbsp duck fat
- 1 tbsp soy sauce
- 1 clove garlic, minced

**Toppings:**

- Slices of roasted duck
- Soft-boiled egg
- Green onions
- Crispy duck skin

**Noodles:**

- 2 servings fresh ramen noodles

**Instructions:**

1. Heat chicken broth and stir in duck fat, soy sauce, and garlic. Simmer for 10 minutes.
2. Cook ramen noodles and divide into bowls.
3. Pour broth over noodles and top with roasted duck, egg, and crispy duck skin.

## Umami Mushroom Broth Ramen

**Ingredients:**

**Broth:**

- 4 cups vegetable broth
- 1 cup mixed mushrooms (shiitake, maitake, oyster)
- 1 tbsp miso paste
- 1 tbsp soy sauce
- 1 tsp sesame oil

**Toppings:**

- Sautéed mushrooms
- Soft-boiled egg
- Green onions

**Noodles:**

- 2 servings fresh ramen noodles

**Instructions:**

1. Sauté mushrooms in sesame oil until soft.
2. Heat broth and whisk in miso paste and soy sauce.
3. Cook ramen noodles and divide into bowls.
4. Pour broth over noodles and top with mushrooms and egg.

## Pork Belly and Egg Ramen

**Ingredients:**

**Broth:**

- 4 cups pork broth
- 1 tbsp soy sauce
- 1 tbsp mirin

**Toppings:**

- Braised pork belly slices
- Soft-boiled egg
- Green onions

**Noodles:**

- 2 servings fresh ramen noodles

**Instructions:**

1. Heat broth and stir in soy sauce and mirin.
2. Cook ramen noodles and divide into bowls.
3. Pour broth over noodles and top with pork belly and egg.

**Chilled Summer Ramen**

**Ingredients:**

**Broth:**

- 2 cups cold dashi broth
- 1 tbsp soy sauce
- 1 tsp rice vinegar

**Toppings:**

- Cold sliced chicken or tofu
- Cucumber slices
- Cherry tomatoes
- Soft-boiled egg

**Noodles:**

- 2 servings fresh ramen noodles

**Instructions:**

1. Mix broth ingredients and chill in the refrigerator.
2. Cook ramen noodles, rinse under cold water, and drain.
3. Pour cold broth over noodles and top with chilled toppings.

**Sesame Garlic Ramen**

**Ingredients:**

**Broth:**

- 4 cups chicken broth
- 1 tbsp soy sauce
- 1 tbsp sesame oil
- 2 cloves garlic, minced

**Toppings:**

- Soft-boiled egg
- Green onions
- Toasted sesame seeds

**Noodles:**

- 2 servings fresh ramen noodles

**Instructions:**

1. Sauté garlic in sesame oil until fragrant.
2. Heat broth and whisk in soy sauce and garlic mixture.
3. Cook ramen noodles and divide into bowls.
4. Pour broth over noodles and top with egg and sesame seeds.

## Kimchi and Spam Ramen

**Ingredients:**

**Broth:**

- 4 cups chicken broth
- 1 cup chopped kimchi
- 1 tbsp gochujang (Korean chili paste)
- 1 tbsp soy sauce

**Toppings:**

- Slices of crispy Spam
- Soft-boiled egg
- Green onions

**Noodles:**

- 2 servings fresh ramen noodles

**Instructions:**

1. Heat broth and add kimchi, gochujang, and soy sauce. Simmer for 10 minutes.
2. Cook ramen noodles and divide into bowls.
3. Pour broth over noodles and top with crispy Spam, egg, and green onions.

## Japanese Curry Ramen

**Ingredients:**

**Broth:**

- 4 cups chicken broth
- 2 tbsp Japanese curry paste
- 1 tbsp soy sauce
- 1/2 cup coconut milk

**Toppings:**

- Grilled chicken
- Soft-boiled egg
- Green onions

**Noodles:**

- 2 servings fresh ramen noodles

**Instructions:**

1. Heat broth and whisk in curry paste, soy sauce, and coconut milk.
2. Cook ramen noodles and divide into bowls.
3. Pour broth over noodles and top with chicken, egg, and green onions.

**BBQ Brisket Ramen**

**Ingredients:**

**Broth:**

- 4 cups beef broth
- 1 tbsp soy sauce
- 1 tbsp hoisin sauce

**Toppings:**

- Slices of BBQ brisket
- Soft-boiled egg
- Green onions

**Noodles:**

- 2 servings fresh ramen noodles

**Instructions:**

1. Heat broth and whisk in soy sauce and hoisin sauce.
2. Cook ramen noodles and divide into bowls.
3. Pour broth over noodles and top with BBQ brisket and egg.

**Five-Spice Chicken Ramen**

**Ingredients:**

**Broth:**

- 4 cups chicken broth
- 1 tsp Chinese five-spice powder
- 1 tbsp soy sauce

**Toppings:**

- Sliced five-spice chicken
- Soft-boiled egg
- Green onions

**Noodles:**

- 2 servings fresh ramen noodles

**Instructions:**

1. Heat broth and stir in five-spice powder and soy sauce.
2. Cook ramen noodles and divide into bowls.
3. Pour broth over noodles and top with chicken, egg, and green onions.

**Oyster Mushroom Ramen**

**Ingredients:**

**Broth:**

- 4 cups vegetable broth
- 1 cup oyster mushrooms, sliced
- 1 tbsp soy sauce
- 1 tbsp miso paste

**Toppings:**

- Sautéed oyster mushrooms
- Soft-boiled egg
- Green onions

**Noodles:**

- 2 servings fresh ramen noodles

**Instructions:**

1. Sauté mushrooms in sesame oil until soft.
2. Heat broth and whisk in miso paste and soy sauce.
3. Cook ramen noodles and divide into bowls.
4. Pour broth over noodles and top with mushrooms and egg.

www.ingramcontent.com/pod-product-compliance
Lightning Source LLC
LaVergne TN
LVHW081335060526
838201LV00055B/2669